The Ladybird
BIG BOOK
of
SLIMY THINGS

Written by Imogen Russell Williams • Illustrated by Binny Talib

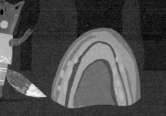

WELCOME TO THE MUSEUM OF SLIMY THINGS!

In the caverns of this museum, you'll find out about all kinds of slimy creatures and plants, things you might think are slimy but aren't, and slime in unexpected places . . .

I love playing with slime!

I don't think we'll be seeing the kind of slime you play with at home here . . .

That's right. Our slime isn't the kind you find in the toyshop – it's mostly LIVING slime, or slime made by plants or creatures. Welcome! I'm Doctor Helena Otterly-Fabulous, and I'm an expert on slippery fish. Mmm, fish . . .

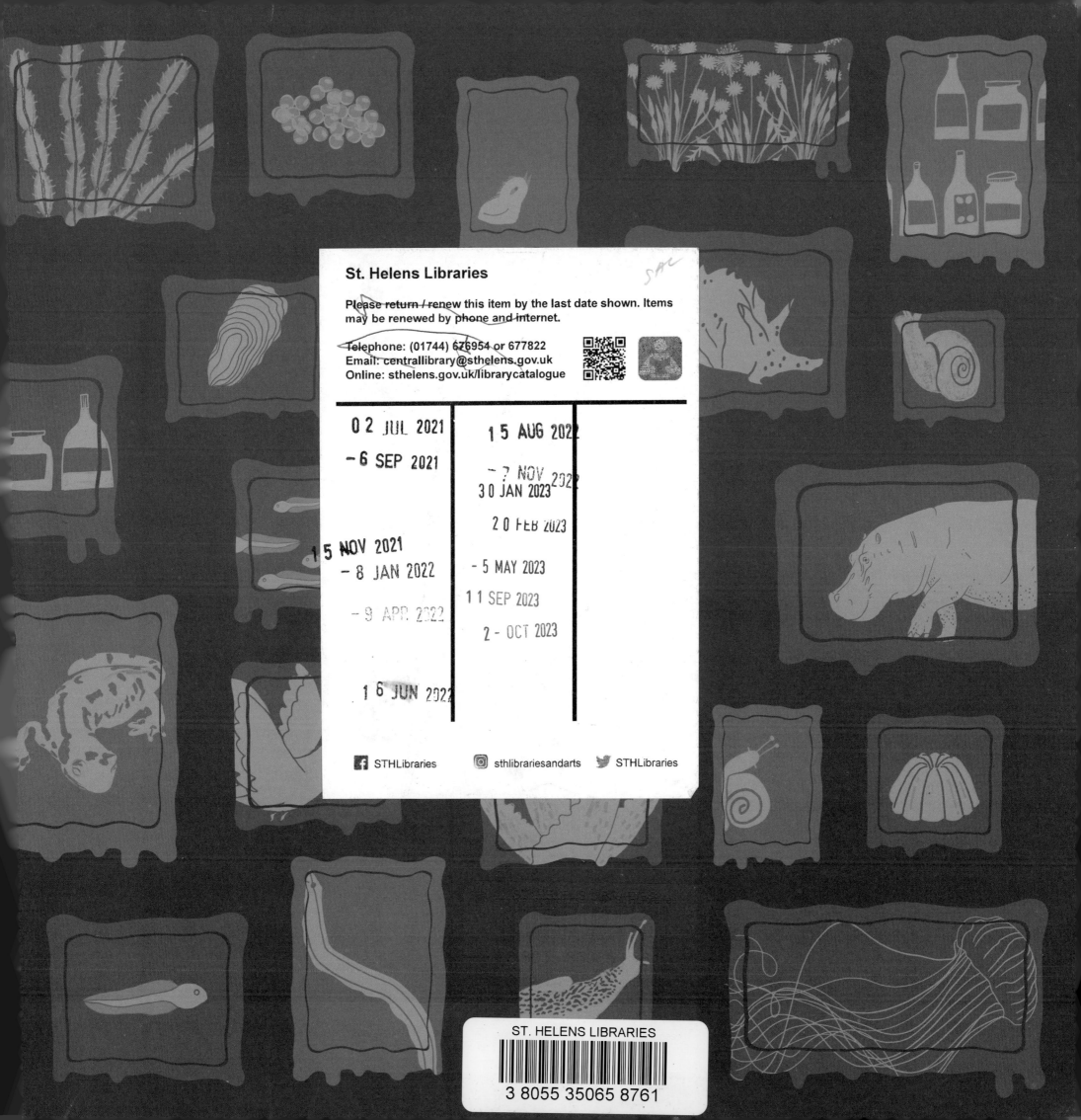

LADYBIRD BOOKS

UK | USA | Canada | Ireland | Australia
India | New Zealand | South Africa

Ladybird Books is part of the Penguin Random House group of companies
whose addresses can be found at global.penguinrandomhouse.com.

www.penguin.co.uk   www.puffin.co.uk   www.ladybird.co.uk

Penguin
Random House
UK

First published 2020
001

Written by Imogen Russell Williams
Illustrations by Binny Talib
Copyright © Ladybird Books Ltd, 2020

Printed in China

A CIP catalogue record for this book is available from the British Library

ISBN: 978-0-241-41362-3

All correspondence to:
Ladybird Books
Penguin Random House Children's
One Embassy Gardens, New Union Square,
5 Nine Elms Lane, London SW8 5DA

THE SCIENCE OF SLIME

In the natural world, slime is used for protection, to fight off predators, battle bacteria and digest delicious food. It's a superpower! (Although perhaps a slightly disgusting one.)

NEWTONIAN FLUIDS

Liquids that stay the same unless there is a change in temperature are called Newtonian fluids. For example, water is the same whether it is in a puddle or in a river, but it will change if heated (steam) or frozen (ice).

Slime is a NON-Newtonian fluid. This means it is affected by things other than temperature. It becomes thicker or thinner when shaken, squeezed or stirred.

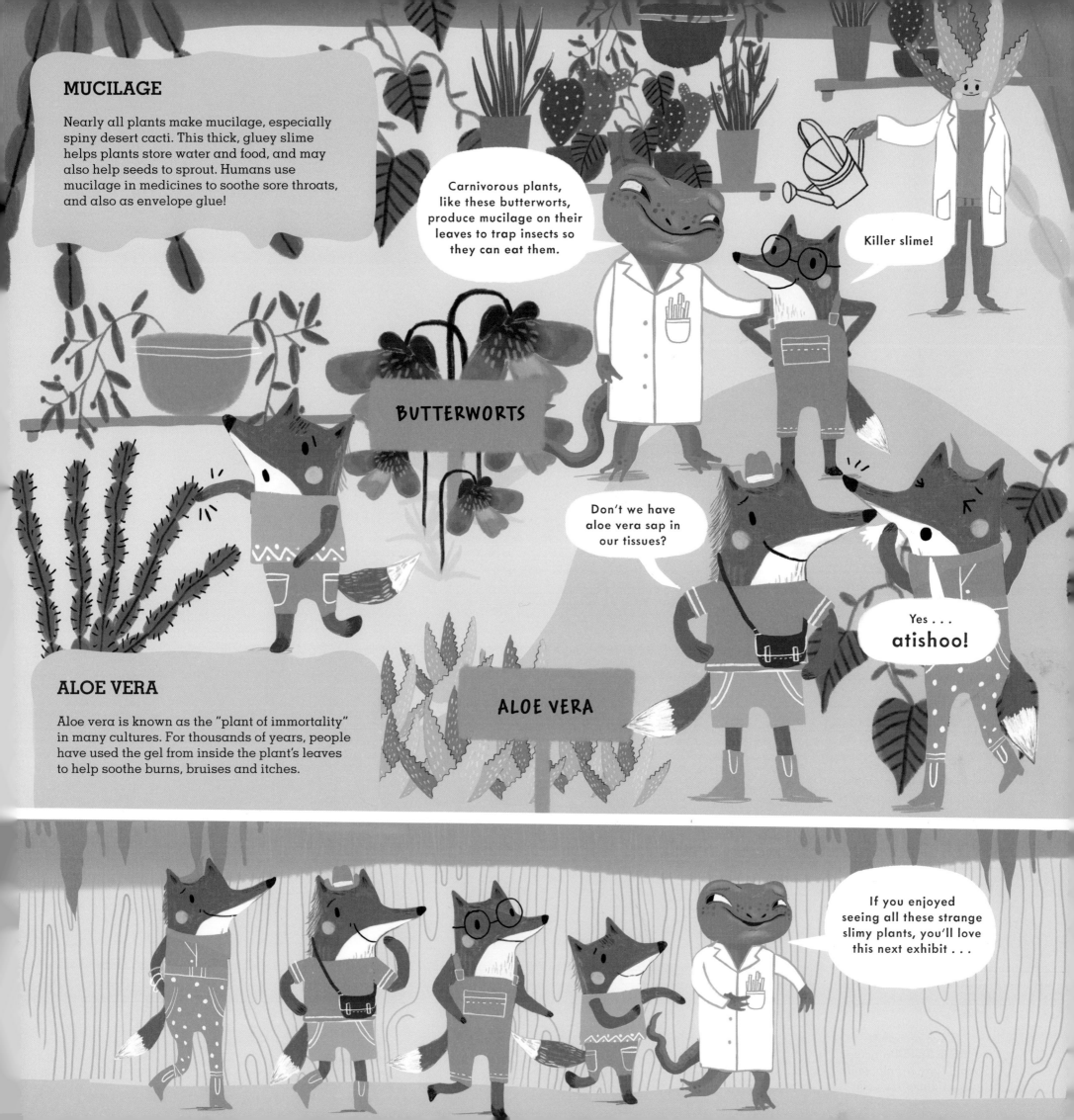

MUCILAGE

Nearly all plants make mucilage, especially spiny desert cacti. This thick, gluey slime helps plants store water and food, and may also help seeds to sprout. Humans use mucilage in medicines to soothe sore throats, and also as envelope glue!

ALOE VERA

Aloe vera is known as the "plant of immortality" in many cultures. For thousands of years, people have used the gel from inside the plant's leaves to help soothe burns, bruises and itches.

THE CAVERN OF SURPRISINGLY SLIMY THINGS

Some things make unexpected slime.
Did you know about these slippery surprises?

HIPPOPOTAMUS

Hippopotamuses create their own sunscreen. When on land, hippos produce a thick pink slime. This not only helps to keep them cool but also protects their skin from the sun.

Hippo factor 50!

VULTURE

Turkey vultures vomit when threatened! These birds use their stinky, slimy stomach contents as a way to distract their predators so they can fly away.

That's disgusting.

PARROTFISH

Colourful parrotfish live on tropical coral reefs around the world. They eat algae and dead coral, and they poo sand! Some species, like the green humphead, can grow up to 1.3 m (4 ft 3 in.) long, and live for up to forty years.

Parrotfish get ready for bed by making a "sleeping bag" out of slime. Every night, they produce mucous cocoons — possibly to disguise their scent from predators.

Comfy!

That's one way to make the bed.

CLOWNFISH

Clownfish live in and around plant-like creatures known as anemones. They have a very thick layer of mucus around their bodies, so they are able to swim between an anemone's tentacles without getting stung.

Why are those orange fish moving in and out of those plant-looking things?

The anemones provide a secure home for the fish, and the clownfish clean and chase off the anemones' predators. It's a perfect partnership!

HAGFISH

Hagfish, or "slime eels" as they are sometimes known, aren't actually eels, but they are certainly slimy. They live in cold ocean water all around the world, and adult hagfish usually grow to be about 0.5 m (1 ft 8 in.) long.

When threatened, hagfish produce an enormous amount of slime. This covers them in a hideaway made of mucus.

Urgh, gross!

Cooool!

They must do A LOT of yoga to be that flexible.

The Slime Salutation!

After the baffled predator has given up, the hagfish ties its boneless body into a knot. It then slides the knot down its body from head to tail to scrape the slime away.

JELLYFISH

Jellyfish are ocean-based creatures that can be found in warm, cold, coastal and deep waters. They have no brain, bones or heart – they are basically slimy bags of water! Despite this, they've been around for 500 million years.

DANGER: BOX JELLYFISH

And they're not actually fish at all – scientists call them "gelatinous zooplankton" instead.

Catchy.

Some jellyfish, such as the box jellyfish, have stings so powerful that they can kill a human in just a few minutes.

Some jellyfish are bioluminescent. That means they can make their own light.

EEL

Eels are long, thin, snake-like fish that live mostly in the sea. Most eels don't have scales – just bendy skin – and they really are slippery to the touch. Eels produce mucus that makes it hard for predators to hold on to them, and in some species of eel this mucus is poisonous too.

The slime on a moray eel sometimes has algae in it, which would explain why this one looks a little green.

Are you sure it's not just a bit seasick?

I read that young eels are called elvers, but sadly they don't have pointed ears, or magic.

You read?

Just popping in! Kelp is a large brown seaweed that grows underwater in forests. It provides food and shelter for many fish and other creatures.

Seaweeds are the salt-water cousins of the algae that grow in ponds and lakes. They can be red, brown or green, and tend to grow in shallow water or on rocky shores, as they need light to make food. Humans use seaweed for food and medicine.

MUSSEL

Mussels are soft, spineless, slippery creatures that live in hinged shells. Mussels use their "byssal threads" or "beards" to fix themselves to rocks. These beards are super-strong and super-stretchy. Young mussels use their beards like climbing ropes to move about on rocks!

OYSTER

Humans gobble up billions of oysters every year, but there's more to these molluscs than food. They actually filter water by drawing it through their gills while they feed. Their mucus then traps extra sediment and algae from the water, cleaning it so the other creatures in the water can live happily.

THE CAVERN OF POND SLIME

Have you ever been pond-dipping? Ponds are full of all sorts of excellent slime. Let's look at some samples!

Can I go fishing, please?

Don't fall in . . .

Scientists have tested the mucus of this Indian fungoid frog for its antiseptic qualities – it's medicine for sore *croaks*!

FROG

Adult frogs are often covered in slimy mucus. It helps their skin to stay moist, protects against infection and helps the frogs escape from any predators. Frogs are also helped to "breathe" by mucus! They have very small lungs and rely on their skin to absorb oxygen from the air as well. Their slime helps to make this possible!

Most frogs have glands on their bodies that can create mild poisons. These are designed to make the frog taste disgusting to predators, and some poison dart frogs are deadly when licked.

FROGSPAWN

Every clump of frogspawn contains thousands of frogs' eggs, all waiting to hatch into tadpoles. The black dots are tadpole embryos. The clear greyish jelly is a nutrient, which the embryos eat until they're ready to hatch.

PARADOXICAL FROG

This South American amphibian is also known as the shrinking frog. This is because its eggs develop into very large tadpoles – some reach up to 25 cm (10 in.) in length. As the tadpoles grow into adult frogs, they actually shrink in size! The adults can be three or four times smaller than they were as a tadpole.

NEWT

Newts spend part of their lives on land, but they always return to the water to have babies. They lay single fertilized eggs, and attach them to water plants. These eggs hatch into larvae and turn into adult newts.

You don't often see newts and frogs in the same pond, as newts eat frogspawn and tadpoles.

SLUDGE WORM

Also known as *Tubifex tubifex*, the segmented sludge worm lives in large groups or colonies. It feasts on the bacteria found in the sediment at the bottom of lakes, rivers, ponds and even sewer lines.

They eat poo?

LEECH

Leeches live mostly in shallow lakes and ponds. They're flat, segmented worms with suckers on each end. Many feed on blood, though some eat insects. Leeches can survive for months at a time on just one meal!

I'd rather not touch that.

It's quite safe. This one had a big meal last September, so it should still be full.

Should?

Freshwater fish in ponds and lakes have special proteins in their skin that dissolve in water to form a slippery slime super-suit. This protects the fish from infection and fungus, and makes it harder for predators to grab them.

So they are sort of like scaly superheroes?

Exactly!

STICKLEBACK

In mating season, male sticklebacks build nests, using "spiggin" (a special mucus). Then they do a special zigzag dance outside the nest to tempt females in to lay eggs. Afterwards, the males stand guard over the fertilized eggs until they hatch.

What responsible parenting!

Do you think they'd babysit for us?

POND SNAIL

Pond snails can "swim" along the water surface, using their shells to stay afloat, or glide along leaves and stones on their slimy feet like land snails do. Some freshwater snails breathe with lungs, and some have gills.

Here are some special snails that live in fresh pond water. I bet you can't guess what we call them . . .

BIG EAR POND SNAIL

RAMSHORN SNAIL

GREAT POND SNAIL

DWARF POND SNAIL

WANDERING POND SNAIL

ASSASSIN SNAIL

RABBIT SNAIL

ALGAE

Algae is the general term used to describe simple, aquatic organisms. They may seem plant-like, but algae don't have roots, leaves or stems. They do create food in a similar way to plants – by using sunlight to turn water and carbon dioxide from the air into glucose (food) and oxygen.

I'll hand you over to Doctor O'Vera – plants are more his thing. I'm all about the fish! Mmm, fish . . .

Algae are amazing! Let's find out more . . .

Too much algae in a pond can turn the water green!

Algae bloom is caused when humans put too many nutrients into ponds, lakes and rivers. This causes high levels of algae to grow, which can quickly overwhelm the water's surface. Sunlight and oxygen can be cut off from the pond, causing harm to the fish and plants below.

So that's what those scummy puddles are in the park!

THERE ARE MORE SLIPPERY, SLIMY, PLANTY THINGS IN THE GARDEN . . .

DANDELION

If you pick a dandelion, milky white slime will ooze out of the cut stem. This wet slime is actually latex, which, in large quantities, can be used to make rubber. The latex that comes from Russian dandelions is strong enough to be made into car tyres!

STAR JELLY

Star jelly is sticky, slimy goo that is a bit of a mystery. It appears very suddenly on grass or branches. People have suggested that it falls from the sky, perhaps brought down in meteor showers. It disappears almost as quickly as it appears, drying up and blowing away in the wind. Where do you think it comes from?

EARTHWORM

Earthworms are known as the gardener's best friend. These slippery animals tunnel through the soil, letting air and water flow freely through the earth, which helps plants to grow.

As they do not have lungs, earthworms produce a slime that allows them to "breathe" through their skin. It also helps them to slip through the soil easily by reducing resistance or friction.

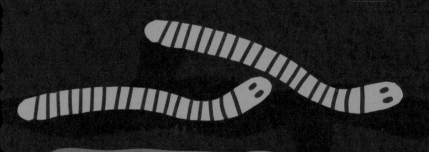

Earthworms eat dead leaves and plants, breaking them down and turning them into compost. "Worm cast" is the scientific name for worm poo. The worm casts make the soil much richer, as they help to return nutrients back to the soil!

SNAIL

Some gastropod molluscs are more commonly known as snails. The name "gastropod" comes from a word meaning "stomach foot" in Latin. Snails have one long, flat foot that they use to move along the ground. This muscular foot also produces mucus, which helps the snail to glide along.

Snails' slime behaves like an oil to help them slide along, and also like a glue to help them scale walls, rocks and even travel upside down without falling.

The thickness of the slime produced by a snail means that it could crawl along the edge of a razor-blade without getting injured.

SLUG

Slugs have the same slimy "foot" as snails, but some slugs are able to move almost twice as fast as snails. Perhaps they're quicker because they've ditched the shell?

Did you know that most slugs live underground? Their bodies are gooey and slimy, so they need moist surroundings to stop them drying out.

Like snails, slugs leave silvery mucus trails everywhere they go. These trails serve a purpose – they help the slugs to find their way back home, like a slippery, slimy map!

Some slugs can dangle from slime, like a bungee. We learned that at school!

Geronimo!

Slugs sometimes make mucous cocoons to protect them when the weather is hot and dry.

GHOST SLUG

In 2008, a new kind of ghostly white slug was discovered in Wales in the UK. Most slugs are vegetarian, but these scary ghosts like sucking up earthworms like spaghetti, then chomping them with their teeth!

THE CAVERN OF FOREST SLIME

You might not think of forests as particularly slimy places, but you can find some magnificent slime-producers here – both plants and animals alike!

SALAMANDER

These amphibians love cool, wet environments. When attacked, salamanders are able to regrow or regenerate limbs that have been lost! Some salamander species are also able to secrete a toxic slime when they're frightened, to try and injure their attacker.

The name "salamander" comes from a word meaning "fire within" in Persian.

Cool! Like mini-dragons!

Well . . . sort of.

GREY FOAM-NEST TREE FROG

These tree-dwelling African frogs lay their eggs in slimy nests. The females produce a sticky liquid, which is kicked up into frothy foam by the males. The females then lay their eggs into the foam for the males to fertilize.

These clever frogs also use mucus to seal their joints and to help them stay moist during the dry season. And, to stop predators nibbling on them, they secrete a horrible-tasting slime as well!

What is that?

The tadpoles are falling from the tree!

The nest protects the eggs for about a week as they transform. Once grown, the tadpoles drop down from their treetop nest into the water below.

THREE-TOED SLOTH

This tree-dwelling Latin American sloth has a very smart – and sticky – green coat. A special strand of algae has evolved to grow in the sloths' fur, giving it a green sheen.

This algae coating is a great food source for the sloth and helps it to hide in the rainforest. Three-toed sloths attract a larger number of algae in their fur than their two-toed cousins.

It's a great arrangement for the sloth and the algae. The "algae gardens" on the sloth's fur get water and warmth, and the sloth gets a free snack and camouflage from predators.

HONEYBEE HIVE

These hives are made up of layers of honeycomb. They are built by the colony – bees use their natural wax to create sheets of hexagonal cells to store food and protect larvae.

ROYAL JELLY

Worker bees produce a special protein-rich gel known as royal jelly. It is used to feed all bee larvae. When a hive is in need of a new queen bee, special cells are built and the larvae within are fed huge quantities of the royal jelly so they develop into queen bees rather than worker bees or drone bees.

TERMITE QUEEN

Termite queens are responsible for the health of the colony and they can lay several thousand eggs a day. The queen releases a clear slime containing special chemicals known as pheromones. This slime tells the rest of the colony who the queen is and attracts soldier termites and worker termites so they can protect her.

VIRGINIA OPOSSUM

Also known as the North American opossum, this animal is the only marsupial found north of Mexico. A marsupial is a mammal that carries and nurses its babies in a pouch. Other well-known marsupials are koalas and kangaroos.

If threatened, this species of opossum will fall to the ground as if dead. It will then foam at the mouth, and jet a stinky green slime out of its bottom for that authentic "corpse" smell.

SLIME MOULD

There are over 900 species of slime moulds. These strange beings can be single-celled creatures or join together as a swarm to create one big "blob" of slime.

"DOG VOMIT"

"EGGSHELL"

"FALSE PUFFBALL"

"WOLF'S MILK"

"THE MANY-HEADED"

"RED RASPBERRY"

Most slime moulds feed on dead or decaying leaves and wood. They can very quickly cover a log or tree trunk in the most surprising colours.

Slime moulds follow their appetite, which means they actually crawl along their food source as they eat!

It's these alien-looking life forms!

What is that smell?

OCTOPUS STINKHORN

This underground fungus feeds on dead wood. It grows inside a white "egg" until five or six red "fingers" burst out! These fingers are covered in noxious black goo that smells of dead things, so they can attract flies.

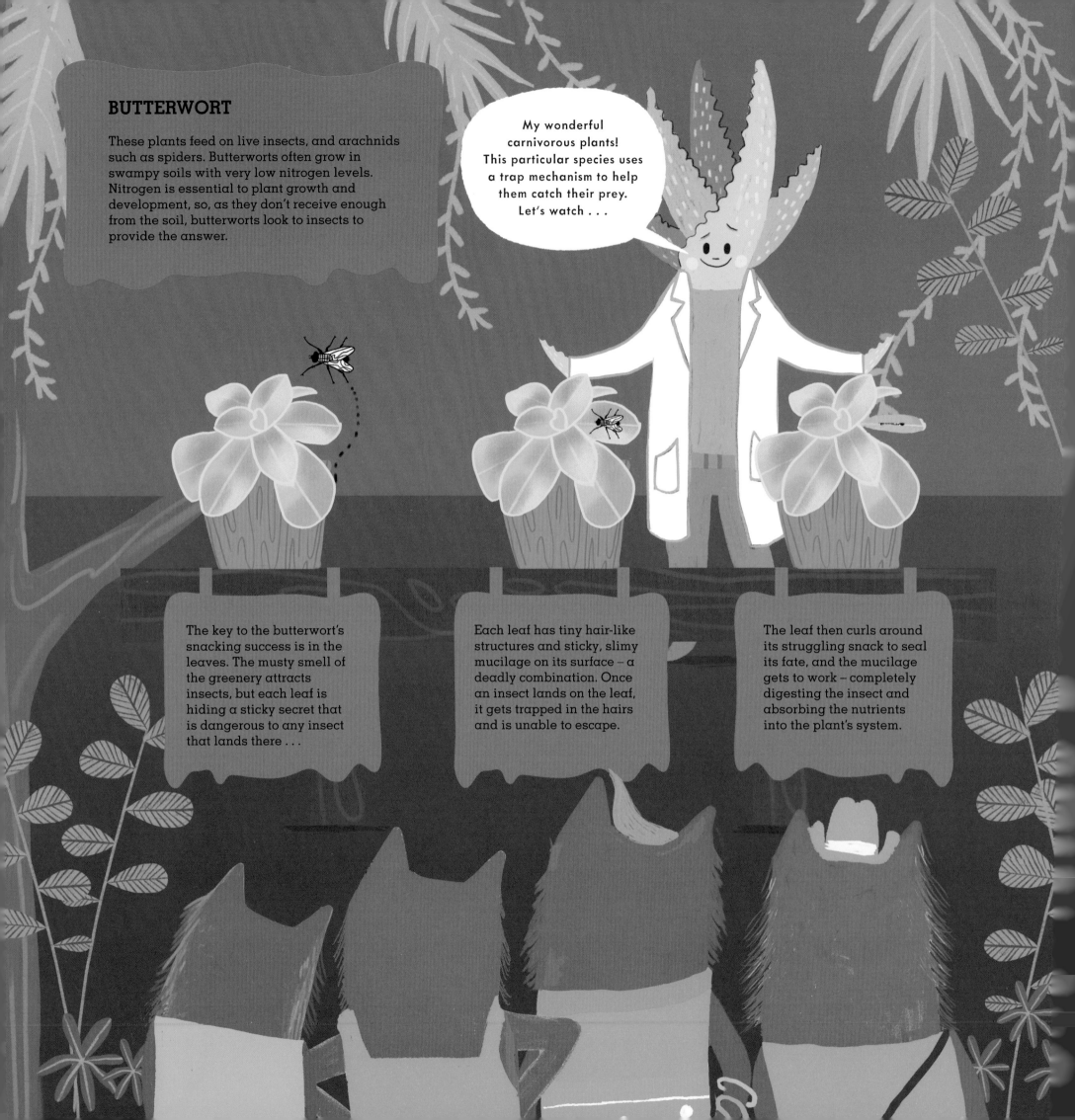

BUTTERWORT

These plants feed on live insects, and arachnids such as spiders. Butterworts often grow in swampy soils with very low nitrogen levels. Nitrogen is essential to plant growth and development, so, as they don't receive enough from the soil, butterworts look to insects to provide the answer.

My wonderful carnivorous plants! This particular species uses a trap mechanism to help them catch their prey. Let's watch . . .

The key to the butterwort's snacking success is in the leaves. The musty smell of the greenery attracts insects, but each leaf is hiding a sticky secret that is dangerous to any insect that lands there . . .

Each leaf has tiny hair-like structures and sticky, slimy mucilage on its surface – a deadly combination. Once an insect lands on the leaf, it gets trapped in the hairs and is unable to escape.

The leaf then curls around its struggling snack to seal its fate, and the mucilage gets to work – completely digesting the insect and absorbing the nutrients into the plant's system.

THE CAVERN OF SWAMP SLIME

People once thought that the "leopard eel" of the swamps in Florida, USA was a mythical beast. Scientists, like me, finally caught and studied one, proving not only that they are real but also that they are not fishy in the slightest. I was really disappointed.

"LEOPARD EEL" OR RETICULATED SIREN

These amazing creatures are a type of giant salamander. They have two front legs, no back legs and a long slimy body that grows up to 60 cm (2 feet) in length. The amazing frill of gills around their necks also looks a bit like a dragon's crest!

Nee-naw, nee-naw!

Not that kind of siren.

SWAMP MONSTERS

Swamps are dark, wet and mysterious places. Because they're difficult to explore, there are legends in many countries about monsters living there. How would you like to meet these creatures?

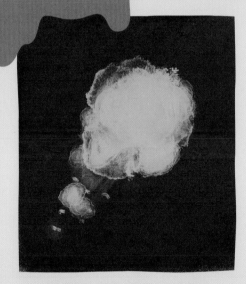

The **HYDRA** is a many-headed serpent whose heads multiplied when they were chopped off. The Greek hero Heracles had to defeat it as one of his labours.

The **WILL-O'-THE-WISP** is a mysterious light that leads travellers deep into marshes until they get lost, or stuck, and are sucked into the mud.

The **SWAMP APE** is a long-haired, apelike creature that gives off a terrible smell! It is rumoured to live in swamps in Florida, USA.

And speaking of mythical beasts . . .

It's you!

It's *totally* your twin.

I think it might be time for a snack. Shall we move on?

THE CAVERN OF SLIMY FOODS

Welcome to my slippery banquet! Do you like eating slimy things, or does the thought make you shudder? For instance, how much would you have to be paid to put slimy food in your mouth?

I'll try slime for free!

A million gold coins.

EGG

Both the white (or "albumen") and the yolk of an egg contain proteins. These give raw eggs their gloopy feel. Egg whites and yolks cook at different rates – this is why you can have dippy eggs!

Mmm, I rather fancy a boiled egg now.

It's the first time I've felt hungry all day.

CUSTARD

Custard is made of sweet cream, which is thickened with egg or egg yolk. The proteins in the egg make the custard smooth and rich – it would pour as fast as water without it!

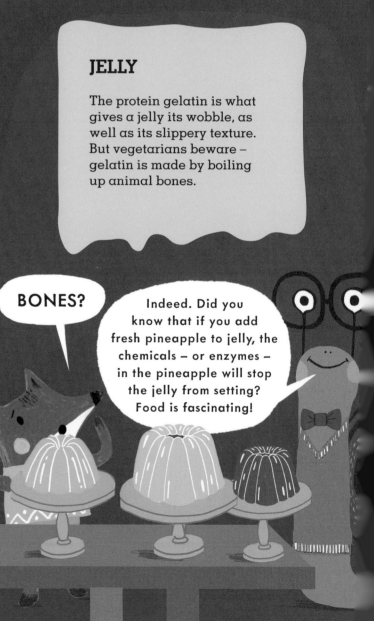

JELLY

The protein gelatin is what gives a jelly its wobble, as well as its slippery texture. But vegetarians beware – gelatin is made by boiling up animal bones.

BONES?

Indeed. Did you know that if you add fresh pineapple to jelly, the chemicals – or enzymes – in the pineapple will stop the jelly from setting? Food is fascinating!

Fermentation can sometimes turn solid food into a delicious and nutritious slimy snack. As it uses a LOT of salt, I might just stay up here . . .

FERMENTATION

Fermentation is a food preparation process that gives food a slimier, gloopier texture (as well as adding in lots of flavour). It uses a good bacterium called "lactobacillus" that already exists in vegetables.

When you chop or grate a vegetable and mix it with salt, it creates a briny liquid that lactobacillus loves! The good bacteria then multiply and feast on the vegetable's natural sugars, turning them into lactic acid.

Lactic acid then gives the fermented veg its tangy taste and creates an acidic environment that supports the growth of lactobacillus and keeps any bad bacteria away.

NATTO is a Japanese dish made of soybeans, which are fermented with special bacteria. It has a strong, earthy flavour, and is eaten for breakfast.

Too early in the morning for me, dear.

KEFIR is made by adding kefir grains, which are full of bacteria and yeast, to milk. It feels smooth and buttery when you drink it – with a little fizz at the end!

Mama says we're not allowed fizzy drinks.

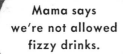

TORORO, another Japanese dish, is a slimy white paste made from grated Japanese yam. It is often served on noodles.

SAUERKRAUT is a sour, tangy food made by fermenting shredded cabbage. It's a well-known German dish.

Sour, tangy cabbage? Umm, not sure . . .

DECOMPOSITION

Have you ever seen a rotting piece of old fruit? The look, smell and feel of that fruit is what we call decomposition. As foods get older, bacteria and fungi react with them and start to break them down. This turns the food into something slimy – and often smelly too!

We have a saying in food science – the older, the slimier!

Natural foods start to decompose the second they are harvested, but they are still safe to eat. After a while, bacteria, fungi and mould will be introduced to the food, kicking the decomposition process into high gear and making the food unsafe to eat.

Decomposition may look or smell disgusting, but it is a very important natural process. It breaks down the nutrients in the food. If the rotting food is then added to a compost heap and returned to the soil, the recycled nutrients can help new plants to grow.

Pee-ew!

Last one to the next room gets a rotten banana!

I don't want a rotten banana.

Why would anyone *want* a rotten banana?

BANANA SKINS – THE SLIMY MENACE?

You may have seen cartoons of people sliding on banana skins. But are they actually slippery enough to be dangerous?

When they're fresh, banana peels are still firm – they haven't yet started to decompose, so you could probably walk on them without too much slippage. But as the peels get older, they will get slimier and squishier. They have less friction or grip with the floor, and will become more of a slip hazard!

respiratory system

skeletal system

digestive system

THE CAVERN OF HUMAN SLIME

But mucus is magnificent! It's an important part of keeping a body healthy.

Urgh! Not mucus *again*!

MUCUS IN THE BODY

Slimy, jelly-like mucus coats the inside of human lungs and sinuses, as well as the inside of the nose, mouth and throat. The hard-working mucus membranes make sure the body has a constant slimy supply as, together, they can produce up to 1 litre (4 cups) of mucus every day!

Mucus is beneficial to bodies. It stops tissue from drying out. It traps unwanted bacteria, dust and pollen, preventing them from entering or travelling around the body. It even contains special chemicals, or antibodies, that fight harmful materials that could make you sick.

I bet my mucus could beat your mucus in a fight.

Are you kidding? My mucus is mightier!

Please don't try and find out.

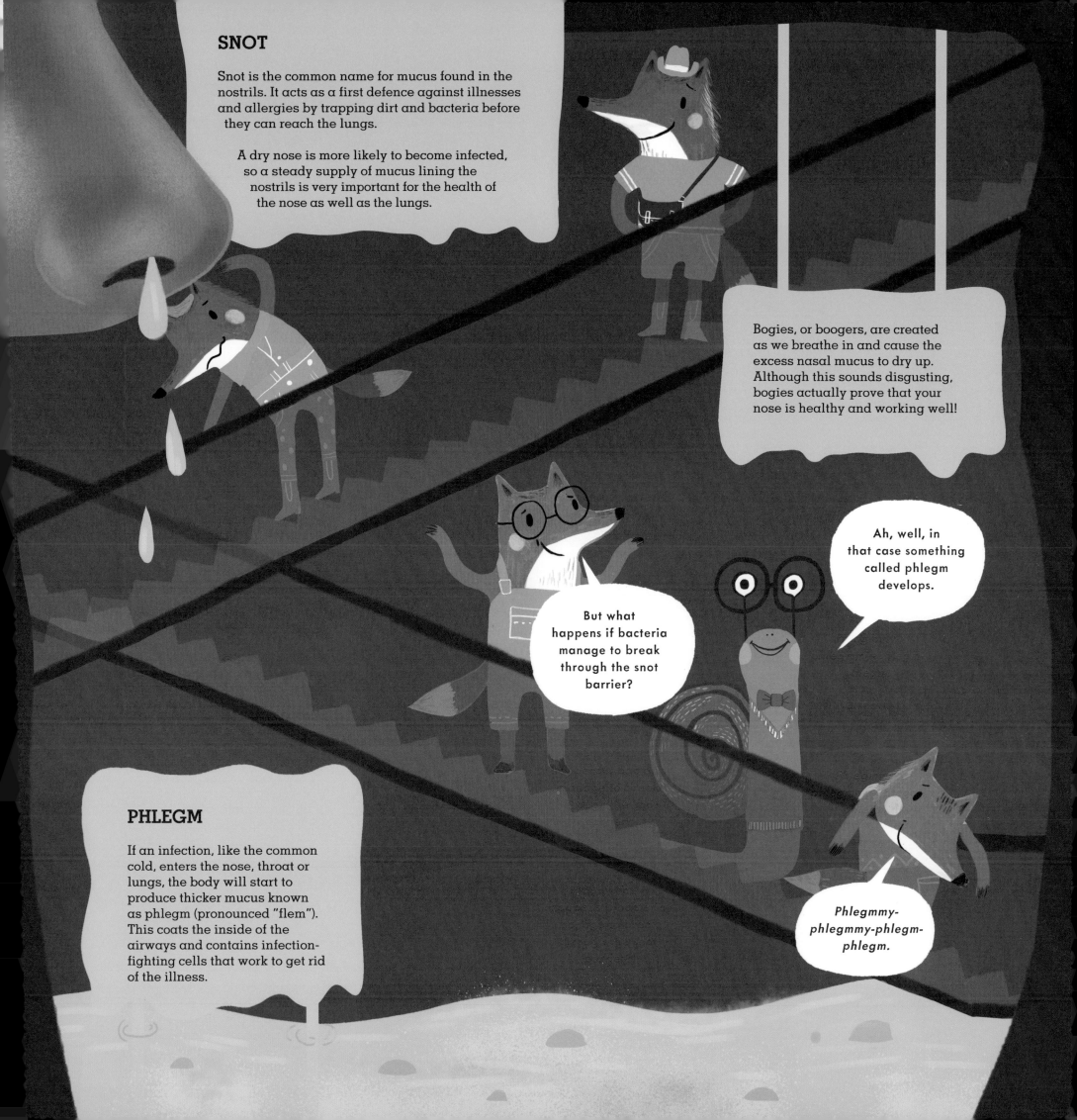

SPIT

Saliva, or spit, is the name of the clear liquid that is produced and found in the mouth. It is mostly made of water, but it also contains chemicals (called enzymes), antibacterial cells and mucus. Mmm, tasty!

Saliva kickstarts the digestion process by making the food we eat wet. Wet food is much easier to chew and swallow, as it starts its 24-hour journey through the body.

Slime also keeps the whole digestive system moving. Digestion is the way a body breaks up food and drink into the vital nutrients it needs. It all starts in the mouth . . .

Teeth and the chemical enzymes in saliva also help digestion, as they break down food into smaller pieces.

Hello . . . 'ello . . . 'ello . . . 'ellooo!

PLAQUE

This sticky, soft biofilm coats the teeth and contains saliva, food particles and bacteria. Leave it long enough, and it will build up and harden into tartar. This can damage teeth and gums, so teeth must be brushed twice a day.

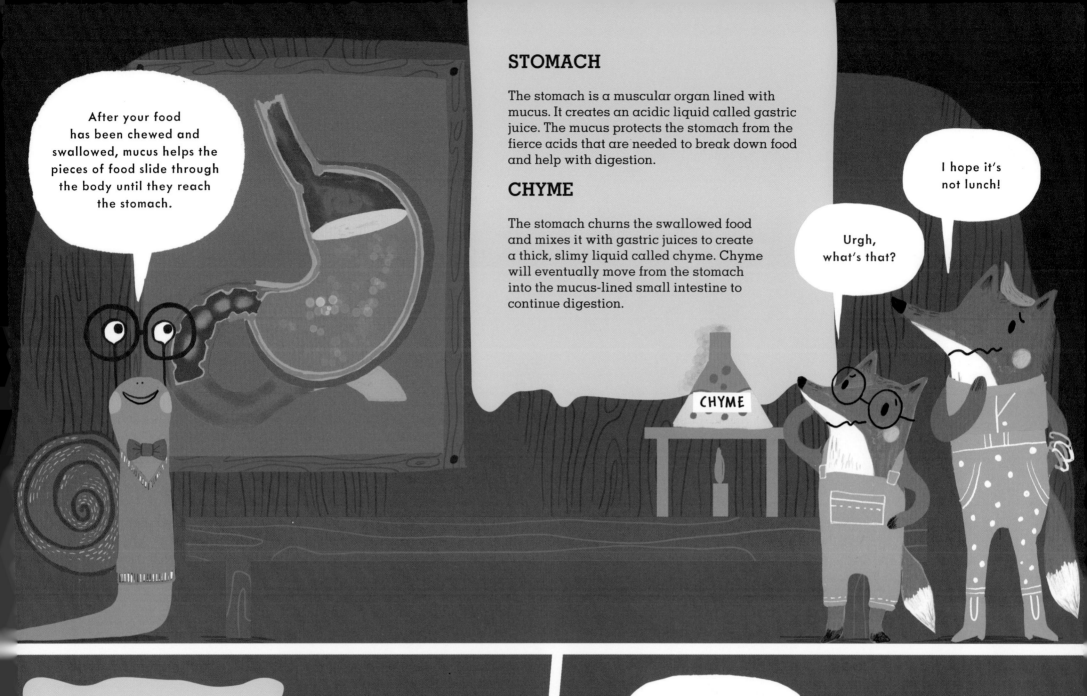

STOMACH

The stomach is a muscular organ lined with mucus. It creates an acidic liquid called gastric juice. The mucus protects the stomach from the fierce acids that are needed to break down food and help with digestion.

CHYME

The stomach churns the swallowed food and mixes it with gastric juices to create a thick, slimy liquid called chyme. Chyme will eventually move from the stomach into the mucus-lined small intestine to continue digestion.

After your food has been chewed and swallowed, mucus helps the pieces of food slide through the body until they reach the stomach.

Urgh, what's that?

I hope it's not lunch!

CHYME

THE INTESTINES

These long, winding tubes are the body's main absorption station! The intestines filter out the nutrients and water from the chyme and take them into the body.

As water is absorbed, the food gets harder again, so the mucus coating of the intestines is needed to help keep it moving through the body.

small intestine

large intestine

So, to conclude, slime helps the body to turn this . . .

Into . . . POO!

Yes, dear.

EYE

The inside of an eyeball is mostly filled with vitreous humour – a clear, firm jelly that gives the eye its shape.

Tears help keep eyes clean and moist so they can move (but eyes are also a little bit slimy!). As well as water and salt, tears contain mucus, antibodies and some oils.

EARWAX

This human-made wax can be grey, yellow or orange in colour. It is made in the outer ear canal, and it prevents bacteria and water from entering the ear.

Earwax actually helps to keep your ears clean – unless too much of it builds up, which can make it hard to hear!

PUS

This protein-rich liquid can be white, yellow, brown or green. When the body has a bacterial or fungal infection, it sends white blood cells to the area of the infection to fight it.

In this battle, skin tissue can sometimes get damaged, which creates a space in the tissue. Pus is the thick liquid that fills the space, and is made up of dead tissue, dead white blood cells and bacteria. Sometimes, you can even see the coloured liquid through the skin.

THE CAVERN OF HOUSEHOLD SLIME

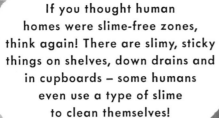

If you thought human homes were slime-free zones, think again! There are slimy, sticky things on shelves, down drains and in cupboards – some humans even use a type of slime to clean themselves!

Slime showers? Cool!

Human houses are full to the brim with non-Newtonian liquids (the ones that change texture when shaken, stirred or squeezed – remember?). The kitchen is FULL of them – tomato sauce, honey, syrup, washing-up liquid . . . this list goes on!

honey   OIL   syrup   soy SAUCE   Peanut Butter   Vinegar

That explains why some humans have a sweet, smelly sheen . . .

There's no slime in MY kitchen!

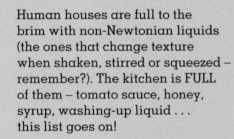

Mmm, tasty slime!

BBQ Sauce   JAM   SUN FLOWER OIL

Shampoo, shower gel, liquid soap and bubble bath are all things used to clean human beings, and yet they have a slimy, wet texture. Some shower gels even leave a light, slimy layer on the skin to keep people smelling fresh!

choc   HAND CREAM   WASHING UP LIQUID   Sauce

Now, let's just take a little peep down this drain, shall we?

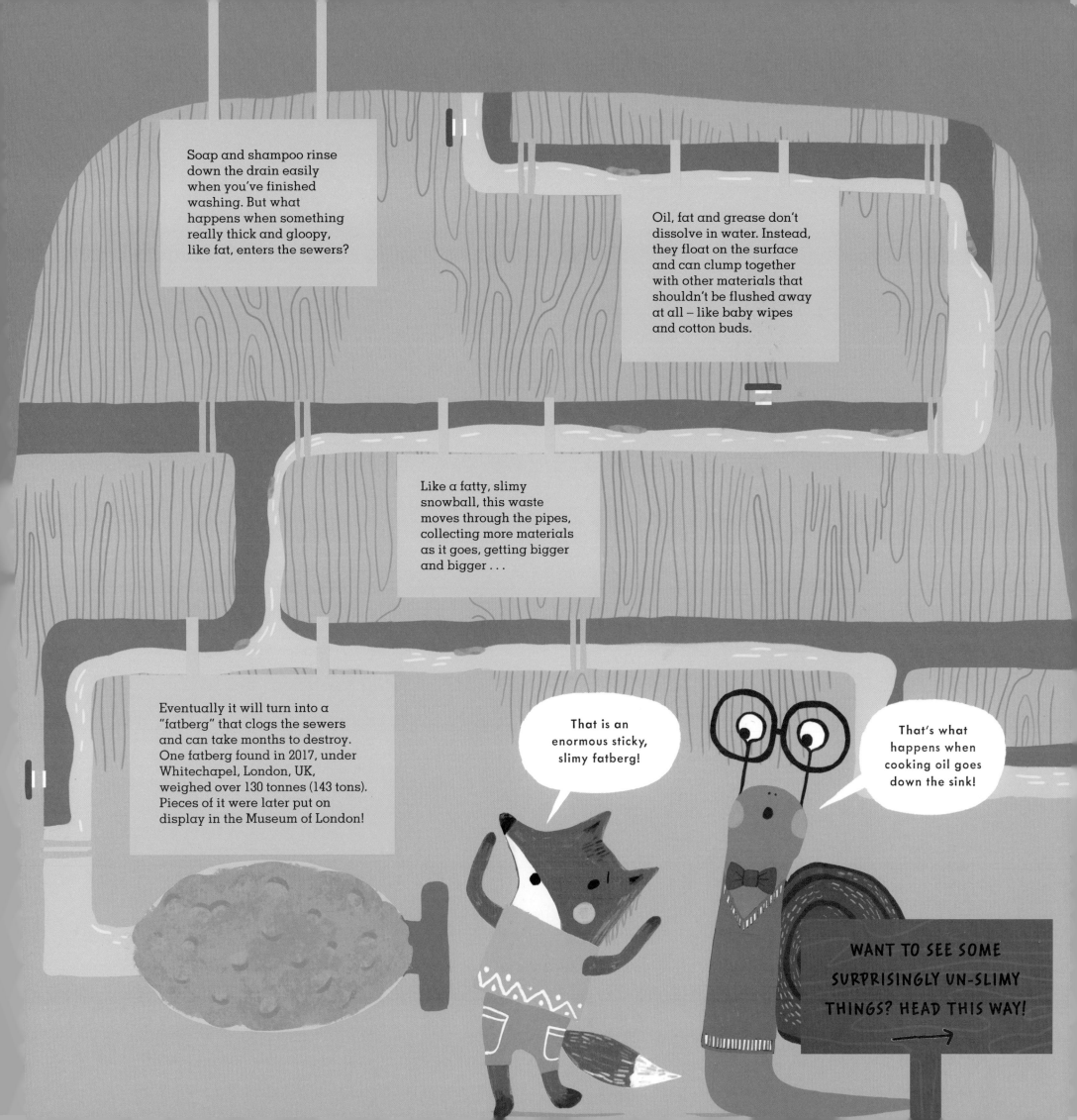

Soap and shampoo rinse down the drain easily when you've finished washing. But what happens when something really thick and gloopy, like fat, enters the sewers?

Oil, fat and grease don't dissolve in water. Instead, they float on the surface and can clump together with other materials that shouldn't be flushed away at all – like baby wipes and cotton buds.

Like a fatty, slimy snowball, this waste moves through the pipes, collecting more materials as it goes, getting bigger and bigger . . .

Eventually it will turn into a "fatberg" that clogs the sewers and can take months to destroy. One fatberg found in 2017, under Whitechapel, London, UK, weighed over 130 tonnes (143 tons). Pieces of it were later put on display in the Museum of London!

That is an enormous sticky, slimy fatberg!

That's what happens when cooking oil goes down the sink!

WANT TO SEE SOME SURPRISINGLY UN-SLIMY THINGS? HEAD THIS WAY!

THE CAVERN OF SURPRISINGLY UN-SLIMY THINGS

Ahhh, finally – a break from slime!

Welcome to the Cavern of . . . er . . . Surprisingly Un-Slimy Things. Lots of people think these things are slimy because of how they look, but they aren't. Let's take a closer look!

Sssssss-smart cars!

I do NOT look dull!

SNAKE

Rather than slippery and slimy, snakes actually have dry, scaly skin, which they shed three to six times a year. The scales on their tummies are thicker and larger than those on their heads and backs. These protect the snake from the ground and help with grip – just like the tread on a car tyre.

Snakes with smooth scales may look shiny or slimy because their scales reflect the light. Other snakes have "keeled" scales, with a ridge running down the middle. That makes the snake look dull, so it's easier for it to hide.

LIZARD

As with snakes, lizards may have a slippery reputation but they actually have very dry skin. They don't have any pores to give off water or oils so their skin stays dry to the touch.

SLOW-WORM

Slow-worms are often mistaken for snakes, but they're actually legless lizards – not worms at all! Their smooth, shiny, grey-golden skin is dry, not slimy. You might find them hiding in gardens in Europe – perhaps under the warm compost heap – as they don't like to bask in the sun.

SHARK

Sharks may look slippery, but their skin is actually rough, like sandpaper – in fact, some human carpenters use it as sandpaper. Shark skin is layered with denticles, or tiny teeth. This turns the skin into an armour, protecting the shark against injury, and helps to make the shark more streamlined.

MEET THE EXPERTS

Behind the scenes at the Museum of Slimy Things, our curators have had a little help from a few experts who are a bit less furry, slippery or newt-like.

DOCTOR HELENA OTTERLY-FABULOUS

DOCTOR HAL O'VERA

DOCTOR ISAAC NEWT

PROFESSOR IVOR SHELLON

Assistant to Doctor Helena Otterly-Fabulous

Doctor Shannon Leone Fowler

Shannon is a marine biologist, studying life in the sea. Her PhD research explored how young Australian sea lions learn to dive, and she has since studied killer whale communication in the San Juan Islands and Weddell seal populations in Antarctica. She's written a variety of nonfiction about the ocean and works as a marine biologist all over the world. Originally from California, she now lives in London with her three children, who want to either be scuba divers or mermaids when they grow up.

Assistant to Doctor Isaac Newt

Doctor Nick Crumpton

Nick is neither a sloth nor a lizard, but he's interested in both. He's a zoologist, which means he studies animals, and has a PhD in zoology and animal biology and an MSc in palaeobiology – that is, the biology of long-dead things. He's worked for the Royal Society and the Zoological Society of London, and he's written books about dinosaurs for children, and talked about animals and science on the television.

Assistant to Professor Ivor Shellon

Doctor Suze Kundu

Suze is a fan of all things squishy and sciencey. She is a materials nanochemist, which means that she studies really small science to make really useful things. Suze has a BSc, MSc and PhD in chemistry from UCL, and therefore knows all of the best slime recipes. Although she confines most of her concoctions to the lab or her job at Digital Science, she manages to also share her love of science and indeed slime through public lectures, as a science TV presenter on the Discovery Channel, and as a science writer for Forbes.

MAKE YOUR OWN SLIME

Here's a squidgy, brilliant eco-friendly slime recipe that will compost or biodegrade without leaving anything behind. It's even edible (though it doesn't taste great!). Happy sliming!

You will need:

- 200 g (7 oz) cornflour
- 100 ml (3.5 fl oz) warm water

Optional extras:

- Food colouring
- Biodegradable or edible glitter

WARNING!

Please make sure you ask a grown-up for permission or for help before starting on the slime.

1. In a big bowl, slowly add the warm water to the cornflour, mixing it in with a spoon – or your fingers.

2. When your slime is as gloopy as you want it to be, stir through any extras, like glitter and food colouring – maybe green for snot, or violet for unicorn poo.

3. Keep your slime in a container with a lid to stop it drying out!

If you're making slime at home, please don't use glue – it turns slime into plastic, which doesn't decompose, and could easily end up in rivers or oceans, making wildlife ill.

How does your slime behave when you let it drip off your hands – or when you squash it between them?

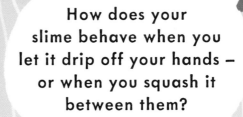